SPLASH!

A HISTORY OF SWIMWEAR

RICHARD MARTIN AND HAROLD KODA

RIZZOLI
NEW YORK

Splash! has been published on the occasion of an exhibition at the Fashion Institute of Technology, New York, June 29–September 15, 1990.

First published in the United States of America in 1990 by
RIZZOLI INTERNATIONAL PUBLICATIONS, INC.
300 Park Avenue South
New York, NY 10010

Library of Congress Cataloging-in-Publication Data
Martin, Richard
    Splash!: A History of Swimwear / Richard Martin and Harold Koda.
        p.   cm.
    1. Bathing suits—History.   I. Koda, Harold.   II. Title.
    GT2077.M37   1990
    391—dc20   89-43564
        ISBN 0-8478-1186-7   CIP

Designed by Charles Davey
Composition by David E. Seham Associates, Metuchen, New Jersey
Printed and bound in Japan by Dai Nippon Printing

PRECEDING PAGE:
Johnny Weissmuller at the Roney
Plaza pool, Miami Beach, Florida,
c. 1929. Unknown photographer
for U.P.I. Courtesy The Bettmann
Archive.

CONTENTS

INTRODUCTION

Splash! is a story about a century's clothing in the one category that goes from land to water with amphibious delight and unceasing fascination. But it is also a speculation about image, for although the fact of swimwear is nothing more than textile, a tangible and retinal truth confirmable by touch and sight, its image involves a decision and sense of adventure pertaining to place, body, and social values—in which the viewer is necessarily engaged. And just as we see the earth's curve from the ocean's shore and view the mountain pool as our own reflection, deepened as a cryptic, answering other, so swimwear becomes object, metaphor, and ideal, taking on an enticing, enthralling form as it is viewed from the water's edge.

Wordsworth saw the swan on the still lake as the twin beauty of bird and shadow. Likewise, we best look at ourselves and beyond our terrestrial cave in water's glowing, showing mirror.

LEFT:
Sky-blue Spandex maillot with criss-cross straps by Anne Klein for Penfold. Photograph by Rico Puhlmann. Published *Harper's Bazaar,* January 1976. Courtesy The Hearst Corporation.

FOLLOWING PAGES:
Underwater swimmer, Esztergom, Hungary, 1917. Photograph by André Kertész. Courtesy Association Française pour la Diffusion du Patrimoine Photographique.

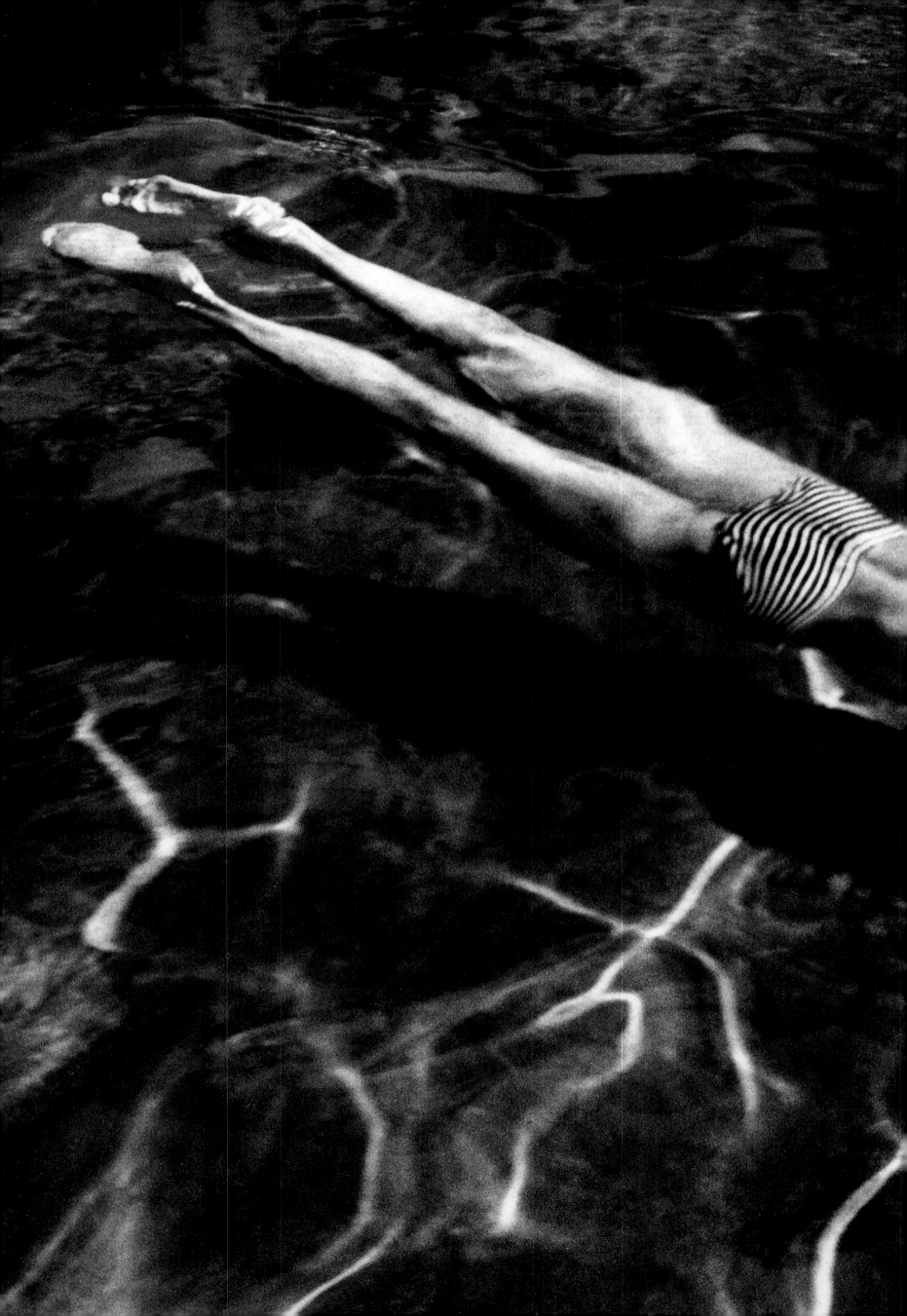

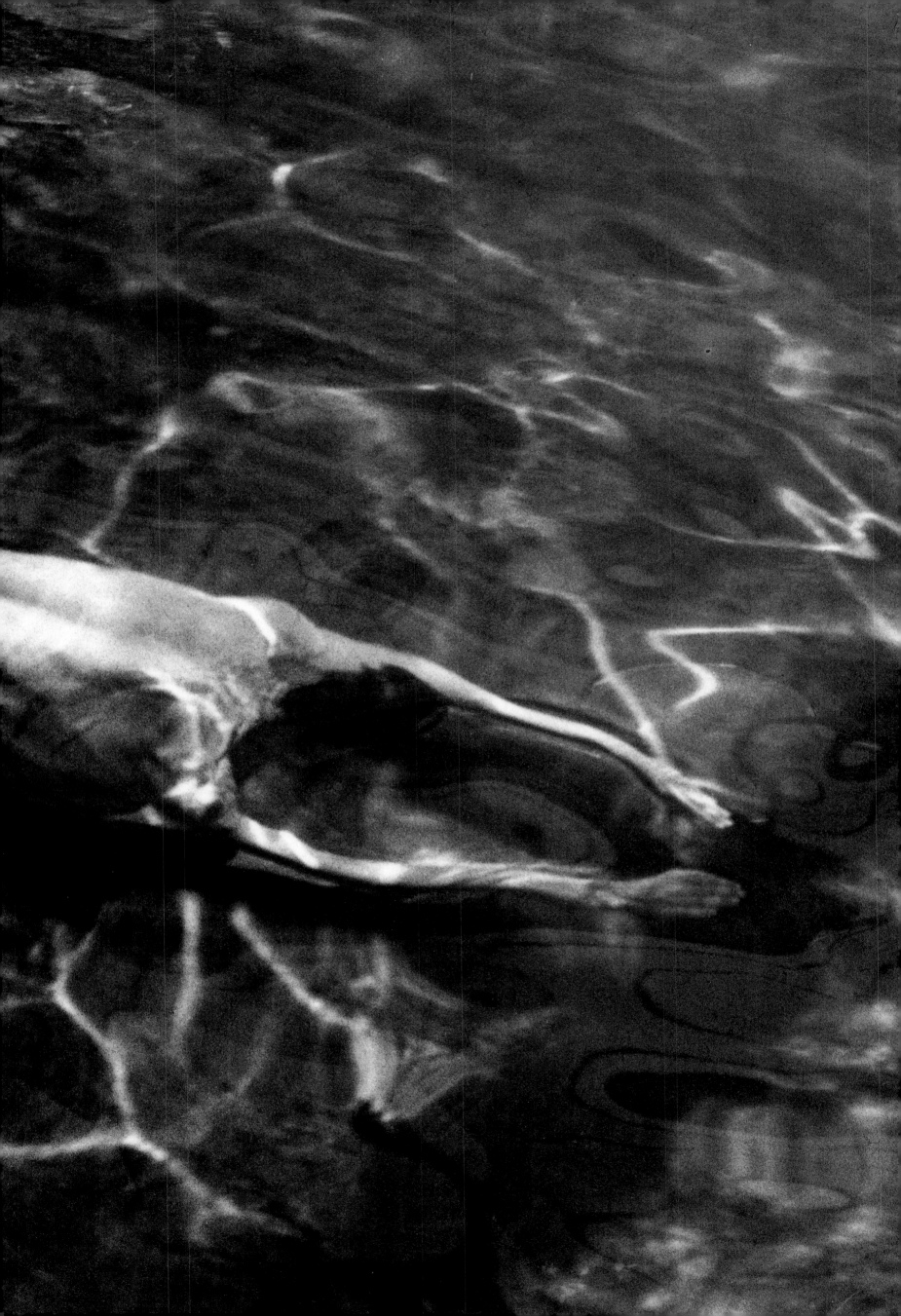

ABOVE:
Ava Gardner, 1943. Unknown
photographer for MGM. Courtesy
The Kobal Collection.

PRECEDING PAGES:
Marilyn Monroe, c. 1950.
Photographer unknown. Courtesy
The Kobal Collection.

T H E   S I R E N S

Inhabited by legions of beckoning mermaids and sirens, and by silently signalling Tadzio on the Lido, awakened by a night sound and shimmer, trembling with the transitory ripple of the bird plundering its prey from just below the waterline, sparkling through a Busby Berkeley film, heroic in the grace of Ederle or Weissmuller, pure as baptism, the Narcissus picture plane of water is everlastingly reflective, its pools ever fresh and translucent, its promise of youth, its refreshment, an unceasing recreation, a re-creation of womb-life before external life, a re-creation of amphibian ancestors, and even the ultimate recreation of the splash that is the joy of bathing. The odes, romantic paintings, and grandiloquence expended on water have been the bane of undergraduate courses and the zenith of artistic achievement. The dream of *Splash!* is not merely a summer's memory or a child's plunge, but that redoubtable douse that is at the heart of the modern imagination.

The control of water has been, since the time of Noah, a mandate upon human beings. The triumphs of the great waterways and irrigations and of those great Roman fountains that revel in the sufficiency of precious stuff gaily tossed into the air in a concupiscence of sounds and of playful cascades are the water music of history. Our visual imagination causes every fountainhead river god and every Galatea in statue to spring to life as at the touch of a plashing Pygmalion of spraying water— a Darryl Hannah of stone transmogrified to flesh.

The circumstances of bathing are complex. The spiritual and healthy waters of the spa promise metamorphosis or amelioration. Beaches have changed in fashion and associations over time and with long tides of evolving values, but there seems always to be a Cannes, a Cape May, or a Malibu in some form. The synthetic sites of bathing are equally important, whether the packaged above-ground backyard pool, the grand pools of ocean liners and cruise ships, or those great bathing places of Antiquity, the public baths. These last were meeting places, expressions of civic pride, and the glory of the plenitude of water. If we can see the vast distance at water's edge as well as our most introspective likeness, perhaps we also speak to the waves, ripples, or placid surface with the eloquence of Demosthenes, an oratory begot at the verge of the splash.

To be sure, our *Splash!* is more than a chronicle of the attire worn to the beach or pool in our century, for clothing reveals— in every way—a great deal about our encounter with the water. Rather, it is about modes in which we in the twentieth century have reiterated ancestral actions but have also confronted ourselves. We have done so as directly as the legendary Narcissus, for whom the watery reflection was a bright mirror and opportunity for self-ardor. We imagine this tale with some slight variation, not as dire as his subsequent sister Ophelia's dive, but as one of happy abandon. Having come so close to the shimmering edge of self-discovery, having faced so directly his definition of beauty, could Narcissus have been satisfied perching at water's edge? Or are we not equally sure that this story, too, like that of Hamlet's naiad, must, in the swoon that accompanied love, the discovery of beauty, and a summer's gleam on the water, be the irresistible *Splash!* that is a tale in itself.

OF FLESH AND WATER

In the 1930s, swimming and swimwear achieved their watershed. Swimming was acceptable behavior, its ladylike etiquettes still up to some dispute, but largely resolved. Less clear in this decade was the protocol of men, though the prominence of male swimmers as early as Johnny Weissmuller at the 1924 Olympics had initiated a long succession of male heroes. Competitive swimming played a role in justifying the male undress, as did the striving of men and, to a degree, women for the newly promoted beauty of the healthy suntan. Reasserting the convention of Egyptian Pharaonic art for bronzed men and for women only partially protected from the sun, swimming for men moved rapidly from competition to celebration. Hollywood's men went topless in the 1930s (though airbrushed into the 1950s to avoid the brutality of body hair), and the nationwide trend, expressing physique while suggesting sensuality, followed with alacrity. Hollywood realized that though movies could talk, few conversations equalled the unutterable sex appeal of cinema flesh.

Fashion magazines contributed substantially to the evolution of women's swimwear of the period. In the divergence between men's and women's bathing attire that was then taking place, men's hewed to sports, while women's was increasingly aligned with fashion, becoming a featured item of haute couture apparel and of the fashion magazines at least semiannually, for summer and resort collections. If men's swimwear seemed to be reaching stability, women's swimwear was constantly undergoing profound changes encouraged by technologies of fabric and construction and fostered by fashion itself. Beach robes and other cover-ups associated with swimming became even more important in the 1930s.

Most importantly, fashion magazines wrought their characteristic transformation on women's swimwear: they created icons and a visual system. Thus, a now-famous photograph by George Hoyningen-Huene of bathers first published in *Vogue* (July 15, 1930) poses two on a narrow board that is the diving board's projection into incalculable space. The measureless space these bathers survey is in contrast to the definite space they occupy, indeed secure by firm, almost frightened grips on the supporting board. They are anonymous in their distant gaze, ambiguous in the likelihood of a studio setting, and so classical that William Ewing has, in *The Photographic Art of Hoyningen-Huene* (1986), perceived a connection to Picasso's *Pipes of Pan* (1923). In all these aspects, the photograph embodies the metaphor that Hoyningen-Huene, Martin Munkacsi, and Louise Dahl-Wolfe generated of the swimmer in the 1930s.

Huene, whose search for exquisite beauty led him to Africa and Greece, but whose odyssey to places never matched the realm of images he created for *Vogue*, endowed fashion photography with the clarity of content and aesthetic objective that we associate with painting. Are we then to consider such swimwear wanderers the counterparts to Picasso's Blue and Rose Period travellers on ambiguous shores? Far from denying the 1930s

ABOVE:
Swimwear by Lucien Lelong.
Photograph by George Hoyningen-
Huene. Published French *Vogue*,
1928. Courtesy the Frederick R.
Koch collection, Harvard Theatre
Collection.

ABOVE:
Jane Russell in a palm-frond print.
Photograph by Martin Munkacsi.
Published *Harper's Bazaar,* May 1941.
Courtesy The Hearst Corporation,
Joan Munkacsi, and Photofind Gallery.

RIGHT:
Jean Harlow, early 1930s. Unknown
photographer for MGM. Courtesy
The Kobal Collection.

swimmer her or his eroticism, one may extend the first-impression sensuality of the swimmer by a renewed sensibility for the water as a place of art's reflection.

After all, the erotic bather was being promulgated by swimwear manufacturers, beauty-pageant promoters, and the Hollywood glamour machine. Submerged chorus lines and splashy synchronized swimming became one of the soft-core pornographies of that decade and the next. Young contract players for the Hollywood studios were routinely posed by swimming pools, in swimming attire, or both, for body-conscious and voluptuous photographs. If Lana Turner, Jane Russell, and Rita Hayworth were portrayed as enjoying the private pools of Los Angeles, the growth of municipal pools, augmented by countless "Y" pools and swimming instruction, brought the swimming pool

ABOVE:
Lana Turner, c. 1940. Unknown
photographer for MGM. Courtesy
The Kobal Collection.

to small-town America, often with the sophisticated mechanisms of the Bedford Falls gym-and-dance floor that opened over a pool in Frank Capra's *It's a Wonderful Life* (1946). Swimming became in the 1930s a Capra fantasy proffered in the hardship of the Depression to those who had once associated it only with the elite playgrounds of Europe and the exclusive precincts of American society. Europe had always taken its waters more for granted, reserving exaltation for therapeutic water. The public pool and open beach, as significantly as the great water engineering of the WPA, brought America a secular Lourdes and a spa for everyone.

ABOVE:

Annual bathing parade, Balboa Beach, California, 1920. Photograph by M. F. Weaver. Courtesy Library of Congress.

RIGHT:

Bathing beauties, 1906. Photograph by Underwood and Underwood. Courtesy Library of Congress.

LEFT:
Jane Wyman, c. 1938.
Photographer unknown. Courtesy
The Kobal Collection.

OPPOSITE:
Gene Tierney, 1945. Photographer
unknown. Courtesy The Kobal
Collection.

Girl on a rock, c. 1930. Photographer
unknown. Courtesy The Bettmann
Archive.

B Y   T H E   S E A

If the well-being of the body was promised by the waters, an aesthetic accompanied the fashion of mind that advanced physical exercise and swimming as healthy pastimes. For nearly three decades, a battle of decency, decision, and decree was fought at the water's edge. In the fourth decade, women's bathing attire changed little in terms of decency, but men's chests became the new field of skirmish. The long civil war of swimwear—a Great War, but fought with different social, cultural, and religious inflections in different parts of the world—was to some an Armageddon of decency and to others an opportunity to find physical expression suitable to a modern world. Women's arms were liberated in the teens; legs were progressively exposed in the 1920s; some décolletage appeared in the 1930s; fiber and fabrics allowed the body beneath to come out in the 1930s and 1940s; two-piece suits and maillots with apertures bared midriff and sides in the 1940s and 1950s; the navel was exposed in the late 1960s and 1970s; high cuts revealed hips in the 1970s and radical gestures even revealed breasts and buttocks. Anatomy was not destiny, but a map of social desire.

Swimwear has served throughout the century to establish and represent standards of beauty and morality. Swim clothing serves this role supremely, not just because it can exchange dress and undress in the twinkling of a cabana or locker, but because water and the beach are the great proscenium of twentieth-century dress. They are nature's runway, abetted by an arch of heaven and the drama of waves or reflective water, and the natural silhouette of clothing worn in the intimate consorting between terrestrial needs and the pure impulse and imagination of swimming.

Spectatorship is as inherent to swimming as it is suppressed as an element of the abstracting, insecure panorama of contemporary life. What we fail to see in the streets, averting our gaze to design and symbol, is palpable at the beach, not only the luminous procession of figures that moves as silently there as on any Greek frieze, but the bright and inevitable joy of observation. A stage for the modern morality play that transforms itself to a theater of the body, the edge of the water is the brink that clarifies all other borders, that illuminates conventions remaining dark on land. It gives a dazzling spectacle of youth, fashion, and attractiveness that is in itself an unending parade of evolving fascination. Music halls, aquacades, and even movie sets might seek to replicate the effects of a plane of beauties posed before an arch of heaven, but nature inevitably offers the grander scene and tableau.

Does the swimmer thus dress in the twentieth century to swim or to be seen? Photography's literal cast shadow is that of the viewer ubiquitous on the white sands of the beach. To be sure, we all know of those who dress for the beach or pool and for the eyes of beholders, never intending to get wet. The diversion and hedonism of swimming is the individual's personal gratification; the spectatorship surrounding swimming is the reciprocal gratification of viewer and viewed. Swimwear and spectatorship are indivisible in concept: in sublime form, the lithe swimmer revels in his or her grace in and out of the water. In aesthetic nadir and pathos, the teeming beach scenes of Reginald

THESE PAGES:
Boardwalk, Ocean City, Maryland, c. 1935. Photograph by Albertype Company. Courtesy Library of Congress.

INSET, LEFT:
Joan Crawford, 1928. Unknown photographer for MGM. Courtesy The Kobal Collection.

INSET, RIGHT:
Playing in the sand at Anna Maria Beach, Florida, November 16, 1923. Photograph by Burgert Brothers, Tampa. Courtesy Library of Congress.

Marsh or Weegee testify to the more workaday bodies that are
equally the phenomenon and spectacle of swimming. Moreover,
countless visual conventions attach themselves to swimming and
swimwear: even studio photographers invented rocks for
would-be sirens; family albums often portray coy flirtations at
the beach; and bathing beauties have formed a long line from
Keystone Kops comedies to beauty pageants to cheesecake and
Sports Illustrated.

Burt Lancaster and Deborah Kerr in
From Here to Eternity, 1953.
Unknown photographer for
Columbia Pictures. Courtesy The
Kobal Collection.

THE SPLASH

Hollywood adored and exploited the bathing beauty from the beginnings of film: by the 1930s, photographs of starlets (male and female) posed at poolside or with the pretext of modeling swimwear were *de rigueur*. Glamour photography and the aura of Hollywood confirmed the beauty of swimwear, even as it approached and became the pinup costume for stars as likely or unlikely as Jean Harlow, Rita Hayworth, Barbara Stanwyck, Esther Williams, and Marilyn Monroe, to say nothing of male figures as photogenic as Ronald Reagan. Hollywood's pinup bathers disappeared only in the late 1960s and 1970s, as more illicit behavior and more than swimsuited exposure became available: skin magazines and movies themselves made the earlier imagery obsolete. After all, a graphic video of Rob Lowe may render less necessary a bashful beside-the-pool photograph.

Like the epochal scene of Burt Lancaster and Deborah Kerr in *From Here to Eternity* (1953), the narrow chasm between recreation and convention is brightly illumined and provocative. Long before the 1950s stars trysted on the beach, the erotic entertainment of the shore existed, even for the early-century straw-hatted men and chastely dressed women who posed for photographs at the beach. The camera's early presence there was a defining fact of two leisures, swimwear and photography, both popular and both defining artistic beauty as well as the most popular forms of same. If, in an exuberant stereopticon image, a male figure rises out of the water to toss his female companion high in the air, the effect is not the misogyny that would be its counterpart on dry land, but rather the clear enthusiasm and cinematic zest for the water of both the man and the woman. Swimming is a social provocation, an edge that may allow for slightly naughty, covertly sensuous behavior. In fact, those who in the nineteenth century saw the beach as a place of indulgence and iniquity were not entirely wrong; others have simply preferred to answer the siren songs of lively behavior and even livelier imagination at the water's edge. Floating and splashing serve as visual conventions for ecstasy, the liquid pleasure of the water, and the freedom from earthbound constraint.

Photography documented with remarkable acuity the rise of the popular resorts that followed upon the increased free time of the early years of the century. Such sites as Atlantic City and Newport now opened to the middle classes of the Atlantic northeast, as did similar recreational sites from Lake Michigan and its urban waterfront to the beaches of California. Where first-phase industrialism had utilized every water resource and founded its cities upon access to water, by the early part of the twentieth century, the waterfront was exploited for the joys of recreation. Much that accompanied such resorts was inherently vulgar or quickly became tawdry, for the beach was only one site of activity. The boardwalk, with its games, garish entertainment, and even piers of special and gaudy diversions, offered the beachgoing spectators eye-popping promises to match the women and men in bathing apparel. Spectacles of diving bells, diving horses, and diving belles accompanied the salt-water taffy and sweet views of the water from Coney Island across America. Brighton, like the candy of Graham Greene's eponymous novel, impressed its low-rent beach-resort sensibility per-

ABOVE:
In the surf, Wildwood Villas, New Jersey, late 1920s. Photograph by Albertype Company. Courtesy Library of Congress.

RIGHT:
The Three Graces, c. 1920. Photographer unknown. Courtesy Library of Congress.

LEFT:
From an advertisement for "Spud" cigarettes. Photographer unknown. Published *Harper's Bazaar*, March 1935. Courtesy The Hearst Corporation.

BELOW:
Heave-ho, 1906. Stereopticon photograph by Underwood and Underwood. Courtesy Library of Congress.

ABOVE:
Black-and-white Argyle-plaid cotton
maillot by Roxanne. Photograph by
Lillian Bassman. Published *Harper's
Bazaar*, May 1959. Courtesy The
Hearst Corporation.

LEFT:
Khaki brown, taupe, and beige
elasticized wool-knit maillot by Rudi
Gernreich for Westwood.
Photograph by Lillian Bassman.
Published *Harper's Bazaar*, May 1959.
Courtesy The Hearst Corporation.

haps even more forcefully than its status as a royal refuge. While
Europe was not immune to such vulgarity—the Cannes Film
Festival was particularly famous in the 1950s and 1960s for the
paparazzi-gathering ingenues in barest attire—the tenor of European beaches was somewhat more refined.

Today, we still most often refer to a "bathing suit" as the
rubric for swim apparel. Certainly, swimwear today is not a
"suit" by any strict etymology, but the concept of the suit persists
for two reasons. First, the word connotes a complete assembly.
Like the fundament of a decision that Merleau-Ponty places at
the heart of the modern transgression of representation, the
bathing suit is, in every period, the decisive limit of civilized clothing, the *ne plus ultra* of the wardrobe. Primarily and ultimately,

OPPOSITE:
White acetate bengaline suit by Rose
Marie Reid. Photograph by
Derujinsky. Published *Harper's
Bazaar*, December 1956. Courtesy
The Hearst Corporation.

LEFT:
Johnny Weissmuller at the Molitor
Pool, Paris. Photograph by George
Hoyningen-Huene. Published *Vanity
Fair*, 1930. Courtesy the Frederick R.
Koch collection, Harvard Theatre
Collection.

OPPOSITE:
Left: striped 1920s-style tank suit by
Ally Capellino. Right: white-belted
black suit by Gazelle. Photograph
by Nick Baratta. Published
Sportswear International, Summer
1990. Courtesy the photographer.

clothing's decency and the body's beauty are only cultural deci-
sions, not universal morality. If there has been such a long civil
war over swimwear, clearly it has not been because of the mo-
ments of revelation at the beach, but because those beaches
stretch back to the streets and communities and cities in their
definition of the proper. Perhaps more importantly, a suit em-
phasizes tailoring and silhouette, and it is these characteristics—
across gender—that remain supremely important in swimwear.
Scant as it might be, as unconstructed as it was to become in
terms of padding and corsetry, the swimsuit is always a legerde-
main of tailoring, a garment that bespeaks its place in the tailored
closet. Fabrics change rapidly with the most aggressive and am-
bitious technology of almost any classification of clothing, but
swimwear continues to call itself the "suit," a tailored assembly
for the body—if often the minimum for its coverage.

What is good for the gander is the same idea of the suit.
Men's early-century attire had appeared reductive: a top covered
the shoulders, but permitted movement of the arms, and body-
hugging leggings could be rolled up from the knee. What was es-
sential, however, was that this functional outfit not be confused
with the patent indecorum of swimming in one's underwear. Indeed, the self-conscious suit elements of men's swimwear, including superfluous belts and buckles and bright striping unlike any
found in underwear, were introduced explicitly in order to differ-
entiate swimwear from underwear. Ironically, the very men who
wore such swimwear likely still equated the women's swimwear-
as-underwear of saucy French postcards with the lingerie and
other erotic vestiary fantasies of the Edwardian era.

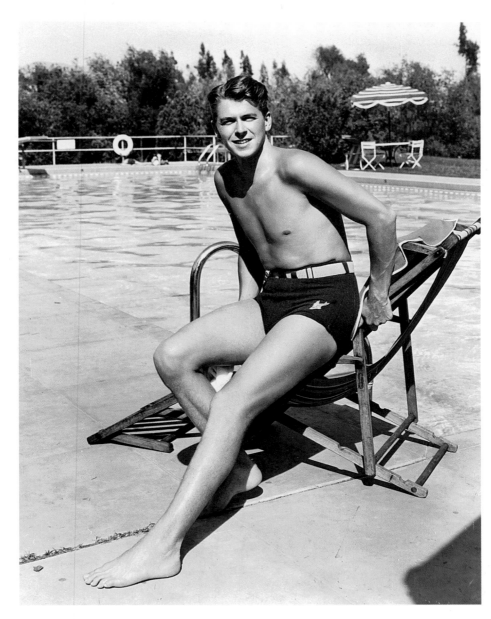

ABOVE:
Ronald Reagan, 1938. Unknown
photographer for Warner Bros.
Courtesy The Kobal Collection.

LEFT:
Tank suits by Issey Miyake, 1988.
Photograph by Cynthia Hampton.
Courtesy the designer.

ABOVE:
At the seaside, 1935. Photograph
by Éméric Féher. Courtesy
Christian Bouqueret, Paris.

OPPOSITE:
Poolside, Berlin, 1929. Photograph by
Martin Munkacsi. Courtesy Joan
Munkacsi and Photofind Gallery.

What the conceivers of the suit strove to suppress was the
natural association between underwear and swimwear, a cogent
and undeniable visual comparison. It was also true that the women's-swimwear industry in its early stages was closely affiliated
with the bra and girdle industry, just as menswear for swimming
was intimately, as it were, connected with the underwear busi-
ness. Only in the 1930s did the technologies of swimwear and underwear bifurcate, as the industries drifted apart with the emer-
gent importance of the West Coast swimwear manufacturers and
the imagery they created out of California, Hollywood stars, and
the new materials and Technicolor palette of swimwear.

The name stuck, but the times evolved. As late as the 1920s,
some local ordinances in America called for women to be fined
and removed from the beach for indecent exposure, including

ABOVE:
Diver, 1929. Photograph by
Alexander Rodchenko. Courtesy
Walker, Ursitti and McGinniss
Gallery.

OPPOSITE:
Pamela Minchin in a Fortnum and
Mason swimsuit on the Isle of Wight.
Photograph by Norman Parkinson.
Published *Harper's Bazaar*, 1939.
Courtesy Hamiltons Photographers
and The Hearst Corporation.

legs without stockings, despite beach shoes and long skirts. Bikinis were acceptable in Europe in the 1950s, but proscribed at family resorts in America. Women's rights, civil liberties, and rapidly changing values conspired to thwart and transform the laws. Beach after beach in America was progressively liberated to allow women to shed their stockings and thereby to begin to enjoy the pleasures of bathing. Skirts were not abandoned, but often cropped and reduced to sheath slimness, as was indeed the style of the period.

Elements of androgyny began to enter the water. Empowered by the swimming command of the water, women required the same functionality of bathing attire as their male counterparts. Thus, 1924 photographs of bathers in the company of their friends show us that women had at some sites discarded their beach hose and were dressed markedly "like the boys," even to the tank tops emulating those the men were beginning to wear. The gender transgression that we associate with high

fashion of the 1920s—Chanel's imaginative appropriations of menswear and the prevalence of sportswear—is also present in the beachwear: even the male prerogative of the web belt with buckle is adopted by some women's swimwear. The geometry and palette of Art Deco in apparel influenced swimwear most especially to assume bright new colors and to move away from the Model-T uniformity of the black or navy-blue swimsuit.

Jean Patou opened his boutique for high fashion swim- and sportswear at Deauville in 1924 and followed up with his shop in even-more-chic Biarritz, so the swimsuit was hardly unknown to the fashionable. Patou differentiated between beachwear and swimwear specifically designed for salt water, thus demonstrating both the practicality of his aesthetic and the vision of the clinging siren as one of the bathing suit's social missions.

If fashion so prevailed even at water's edge, it was because it was a style profoundly fashionable, at one with the largest cultural traits of the era. Swimming was only one element of the 1920s and 1930s craze for physical fitness, one not paralleled until the 1980s. Annette Kellerman was a model sportswoman; individual and group exercises, especially with the salubrious support of sea air, were advocated by doctors, family advisors, and even the etiquette authors and fashion magazines. Health clubs were founded, generally segregating men and women, but beaches and swim clubs for both became places not only of relaxation and promenade, but of jumping jacks, push-ups, and other exercise. Likewise, school and college recreation stressed fitness activities common to men and women, if still chiefly seg-

ABOVE:
Black-wool bloomer suit with a Talon zipper. Photograph by Louise Dahl-Wolfe. Published *Harper's Bazaar*, January 1941. Courtesy Center for Creative Photography, University of Arizona and The Hearst Corporation.

OPPOSITE:
Strong stretch. Photograph by Martin Munkacsi. Published *Harper's Bazaar*, October 1937. Courtesy The Hearst Corporation, Joan Munkacsi, and Photofind Gallery.

ABOVE:
Girls with beach ball on Clearwater
Beach, Florida, April 18, 1924.
Photograph by Burgert Brothers,
Tampa. Courtesy Library of
Congress.

regated for decorum. In demanding more of women on the
beach, the exercise phenomenon required less restrictive clothing and gave a prized result—enhanced confidence in the body
and the desire to reveal it. Youth and new money seized the
imagination of countless designers of the 1920s; freshness clung
to the 1920s as undeniably as mystery generated the aura of
Jay Gatsby in the same period, he to die in his "bathing-suit,"
according to Fitzgerald (presumably, the belted variety with tank
top, underarm scoop, and wool pants down almost to the
knees) in his swimming pool.

American scientific hygiene was transmitted around the
world, its theory finding elegant embodiment and extension in
American expatriates, as well as in a zealous fringe in America,
Germany, and England that promoted nudism and other forms
of natural living as a progressive twentieth-century expression.
The Fascist exaltation of the toned body, manifest in Leni Riefen-
stahl's *Triumph of the Will* (1934), is the sinister side of the discovery of the body in the 1920s and 1930s. Beach balls in bright
colors were replaced for a time by medicine balls and the vigor
of beach exercise. Perhaps no site more readily suggests the
fitness phenomenon associated with swimming than Muscle
Beach, the California strand eponymous with body building and
the bulked, hulking bodies created at the ocean shore. Are these
musclebuilders destined for buoyancy in water sports, or are
they performing their body sculpture and related performance
art for the spectatorship on the beach? The supermen and the
women held aloft at Muscle Beach are seldom in the water;
instead, they are on view. Not every swimmer of the 1920s or
1930s might have sought the Arnold Schwarzenegger *avant la
lettre* posing style of Muscle Beach, but physique was flexing its
muscle in ways that demanded exposure.

ABOVE:
Camille Duvall in a suit by Gilda
Marx. Photograph by Michael
Halsband. Published *Interview*,
September 1986. Courtesy the
photographer.

It was not swimming, however, that brought the chief tech-
nological innovation to swimsuit manufacture in the 1920s. A
ribbed-knit rowing outfit was adapted to swimwear by Jantzen,
resulting in a garment sufficiently cross-bonded to adhere to the
body and allow flexibility. Ribbed knits prevailed through the
decade as the favored textile of swimwear construction. Swimwear was also expanded by the popularity of surfing, which
arrived on American beaches in the late 1920s and 1930s from
Hawaii, largely due to the charisma of champion surfer Duke
Kahanamoku. Likewise, waterskiing and scuba diving expanded
the active options for lake and ocean leisure.

ABOVE:
Hans Hedelmann wearing cotton
and Lycra shorts by Robert
Mannino for Tank Therapy.
Photograph by Aaron Chang.
Published *Esquire,* June 1988.
Courtesy the photographer.

LEFT:
Hawaiian surfing champion Duke
Kahanamoku, August 6, 1929.
Photographer unknown. Courtesy
Library of Congress.

Claire McCardell, Tina Leser, Tom Brigance, and Carolyn Schnurer were among the American designers associated with swimwear, with the great houses of Cole of California, Jantzen, Rose Marie Reid, Elisabeth Stewart, and B.V.D. These continued to create swimwear in one-piece suits, two-piece suits, and multiple elements of complex outfits that layered swimwear to skirts and cover-ups. Compositions toyed with the shapes of umbrellas and the shadows they cast. A Dahl-Wolfe photograph (*Harper's Bazaar,* January 1947) places a swimmer with kerchief at the line of the high tide, her tracks as significant as Friday's, and her shadow long on the sandy terrain above the tidemark. Sun-worshipping maidens in almost ecclesiastical semaphore to the sun (*Harper's Bazaar,* June 1944) by Dahl-Wolfe confirm the contrivance of the outdoors photograph achieved under circumstances of maximum control.

ABOVE:
Twins at the beach, 1955.
Photograph by Louise Dahl-Wolfe.
Courtesy Staley-Wise Gallery.

Popular culture, meanwhile, established its conventions for accepting the buxom movie stars of the time, and fashion photography likewise sought strong conventions for its images of swimmers and all that accompanied swimming. Those conventions coincided in a Dahl-Wolfe photograph of a Claire McCardell swimsuit (*Harper's Bazaar*, May 1945): the fashion figure smiles with the requisite Hollywood smile, places one hand at her forehead in typical cheesecake pose, and stretches the other arm out to thrust the chest forward and to expose it. All the elements of pinup seduction are here, but the soft form of the McCardell swimsuit and even the black-and-white reproduction of the Dahl-Wolfe image mark the great distance between swimwear fashion and its use in promoting Hollywood. Neither photographic genre represented garden-variety swimming, but it was perhaps only by such pictorial embellishment that the visualization of the swimmer might return to the pleasures of the beach and the water without the dour fears of a war that had been defined to the American audience in terms of two great ocean theaters. If the oceans signified war, then the surf or the beach was hardly safe or happy.

LEFT:
Maillot in DuPont nylon and Lycr
Spandex, by Catalina Jr. Photogra
by Oliviero Toscani. Published
Harper's Bazaar, January 1973.
Courtesy The Hearst Corporatic

OPPOSITE:
Esther Williams, c. 1950. Unknov
photographer for MGM. Courtes
The Kobal Collection.

New images were necessary to make it safe to go back in the water. Hollywood helped, with characteristic glee, as did Esther Williams movies stretching into the 1950s, and the possibilities of natatoria and aquacade spectacles that gleamed with film's sumptuous Technicolor. Virtuoso engineering and adaptable materials made available after the war's needs ended offered Hollywood a fantasy of shapes and textures to give postwar swimwear an arresting, if often almost imaginary sexuality, embodying the most inflated dreams of men in uniform conjur-

LEFT:
Kathleen Cassidy in a chintz bathing
suit by Cole of California.
Photograph by Engstead. Published
Harper's Bazaar, December 1947.
Courtesy The Hearst Corporation.

OPPOSITE:
Maillot with pleated overskirt in
black elasticized Alamac jersey, by
Cole of California. Photograph by
Engstead. Published *Harper's
Bazaar*, November 1953. Courtesy
The Hearst Corporation.

ing women in bathing suits. Arguably, high fashion offered the
same in the years after the war with the Dior New Look and
other styles stressing the femininity that had been impossible
under conditions of war and the dream of woman that had
been promoted in the same period. What constituted postwar
femininity was, of course, a coarse exaggeration. In dress, the
New Look fostered extreme notice of erogenous zones, including a tiny wasp waist recalling the days of corseting, the volumi-
nous flare of the skirt, and the thrust of the bosom akin to the
cantilevered architecture of the period. In swimsuits, the conical
breasts, created of wire and padding, were a prominent feature.
Moreover, the new mode of the bikini that might have been
thought to supplant by sheer sexuality the earlier one-piece
maillot was not as apocalyptic as had been anticipated. Both
one- and two-piece bathing suits were options in the 1940s and
1950s, and the cling of new synthetic fibers allowed the silhouette of the swimsuit, whether maillot or bikini, to reveal a great
deal about the bather.

ABOVE:
Douglas Fairbanks, Jr., and Joan
Crawford, Santa Monica, California.
Photograph by Nickolas Muray.
Published *Vanity Fair*, October
1929. Courtesy Condé Nast
Publications, Inc.

OPPOSITE:
Black bikini by Jer-Sea of Sweden,
with striped cotton sun coif by Lilly
Daché. Photograph by Saul Leiter.
Published *Harper's Bazaar*, June
1962. Courtesy the photographer
and The Hearst Corporation.

Johnny Weissmuller in the terry-
cloth robe of the Paris Olympics,
1928. Photograph by Nickolas
Muray. Courtesy International
Museum of Photography at George
Eastman House.

White terry-cloth coverall by Caltex.
Photograph by Toni Frissell.
Published *Harper's Bazaar,* January
1951. Courtesy The Hearst
Corporation.

Tony Curtis sunning in terry cloth,
c. 1960. Photographer unknown.
Courtesy The Kobal Collection.

LEFT:

Martin Munkacsi on fashion shoot, Long Island Sound. Photograph by Paal. Published *Harper's Bazaar*, November 1935. Courtesy Joan Munkacsi, Photofind Gallery, and The Hearst Corporation.

OPPOSITE:

Bathers on Margarita Island, Budapest, 1929. Photograph by Martin Munkacsi. Courtesy Joan Munkacsi and Photofind Gallery.

ABOVE:
Yvonne Printemps at Royan,
Atlantic Coast of France, 1924.
Photograph by Jacques-Henri
Lartigue. Courtesy Association des
Amis de J.-H. Lartigue.

LEFT:
Bathing caps by U.S. Rubber.
Photograph by Richard Rutledge.
Published American *Vogue*, 1957.
Courtesy Condé Nast Publications, Inc.

Silk jersey swimsuit by Emilio Pucci.
Photograph by Saul Leiter.
Published *Harper's Bazaar*, January
1960. Courtesy the photographer,
and The Hearst Corporation.

NEW SEAS AND SITES

But the rubric of art could hardly attach to 1950s swimwear, which stressed a *retardataire* and aggressive femininity, along with such bizarre fads as animal-skin swimwear. Yet, if swimwear was any indicator of fashion, it demonstrated an era in which an exaggerated femininity was expressed; the newly powerful media, including television, promoted rapid fads; and the suburban and casual sporting life allowed for excesses and the exuberant forms of a wealthy nation. Exoticism inflected the settings of swimwear, with the airplane making Hawaii, Mexico, and the Caribbean accessible and thereby advancing a new geography of American swimwear. Dahl-Wolfe, Norman Parkinson, Lillian Bassman, Saul Leiter, and other fashion photographers devised a hybrid between traditional swimwear images and the imagery of place. Thus, palm trees, signs of ancient Meso-America, and other indicators abound; many photographs suggest unexplored tropical paradises.

Exoticism, defined and indefinable locations of lush beauty, and the impression of uncharted beaches and venues became the standard of 1950s swimming, as if to indicate that poolside life, either communal or private, was no longer sufficient for a leader nation that could afford travel as well as leisure. In 1952, for instance, Dahl-Wolfe photographed, surrounded by all the accoutrements of Japanese life, a polished-cotton swimsuit by Carolyn Schnurer that emulated the design of a Japanese paper box. A *Harper's Bazaar* swimwear shoot of May 1955 at the Lido in Gallipoli forgets the fighting and instead remembers de Chirico in the self-conscious use of dressing-room doorways and foreboding shadows to create an image struggle between Milan and Marienbad. A Dahl-Wolfe photograph (cover) of a model in a McCardell wool-gabardine swimsuit of 1946 combines mantric pose, exotic flowers, and the map of North Africa upon which she rests her head. Moorish shutters, turban, and a route adumbrated by the necklace falling across the map are ancillary indications of place. In like manner, Dahl-Wolfe's 1946 photograph of women in kilt swimsuits is exotic in setting, but also implies time travel: the models' short, pleated skirts echo, in texture and length, the garb of the classical figure of the tile decoration, as do their sandals. Swimwear photography now expressed geography as well as clothing and model, and the added attribution of site to most swim photography of the 1950s confirmed that travel was an intrinsic part of the postwar adventure with the sea and swimming.

Scotch-pleat skirts. Left: rayon dress
with matching shorts by Carolyn
Schnurer; right: rayon kilt, bandeau,
and shorts by Duchess Royal.
Photograph by Louise Dahl-Wolfe.
Published *Harper's Bazaar,* May 1946.
Courtesy The Hearst Corporation.

Wool-garbardine suit by Claire
McCardell. Photograph by Louise
Dahl-Wolfe. Published *Harper's
Bazaar*, May 1946. Courtesy The
Hearst Corporation.

LEFT:
One-shouldered, bias-cut black
piqué suit by Brigance for
Sportsmaker. Photograph by Lillian
Bassman. Published *Harper's
Bazaar*, May 1954. Courtesy The
Hearst Corporation.

RIGHT:
On the beach in North Africa. Left:
gray Fairtex-knit maillot with red-
and-white stripes, by Maidenform;
right: royal-blue Antron nylon knit
two-piece suit by Roxanne.
Photograph by Derujinsky.
Published *Harper's Bazaar*, January
1962. Courtesy The Hearst
Corporation.

RIGHT:
Fashion shoot on Majorca. Two-piece black demi-bikini in Vyrene and stretch-nylon knit, by Brigance for Sinclair. Photograph by Derujinsky. Published *Harper's Bazaar*, January 1961. Courtesy The Hearst Corporation.

109

RIGHT:
Swim shorts by Gianfranco Ferré
for Oaks. Photograph by Nadir.
Published *L'Uomo Vogue,* Milan,
May 1988. Courtesy Edizioni
Condé Nast Italia, S.p.A.

ABOVE:
Zebra-striped maillot in Antron
nylon and Lycra, by Sandcastle.
Photograph by Barry McKinley.
Published *Harper's Bazaar,* January
1974. Courtesy The Hearst
Corporation.

Midsummer high jinks in a black-duck
turban by Halston and black-Lycra
swimsuit by Rose Marie Reid.
Photograph by Martin Munkacsi.
Published *Harper's Bazaar*, July 1962.
Courtesy Joan Munkacsi, Photofind
Gallery, and The Hearst
Corporation.

S U N N Y   A N D
S E X Y   I R O N I E S

Despite the bravado of Hollywood exposure, the American and Americanized beaches remained relatively demure through the 1950s, but in the hedonistic 1960s all that had been forestalled and much that had been concealed emerged. The American contentment with modest maillots and demure two-piece suits was rocked by a discovery of the body and a quick catching-up with European bikinis and even one-piece suits that revealed more of the body. To discover new erogenous zones became the origami of swimwear construction. Styles scooped to one part of the body or another, but the most radical and consistent exposure was the navel. Like the rude burlesque of *Laugh-In,* clothing—and swimwear as its *mer*-microcosm—displayed the navel with a playful sensitivity that was infectious, especially for the lithe and "in." The fashion magazines recorded hats and swirling caftans as if they were omnipresent on the beaches (though they were, in fact, hardly there) but they added another possibility for humor and for silhouette. A Munkacsi photograph of a bather in a black Lycra swimsuit by Rose Marie Reid achieves its Isadora Duncan impact from an ample black-duck turban by Halston, just about to make his transition from millinery to apparel. In its rabbit-eared absurdity, the turban brings drama to a photograph of an otherwise classic swimsuit. As if to mitigate the new eroticism, the midriffs arrived at the beach with belly laughs: absurd combinations of fancy dress with informal swimming styles, the antic humor of less and more in dress, and the renewal of the beach frolic as a comedy, almost as if extending the Keystone Kops caricature that had arrived with erotic innovation in the 1920s.

But the real swimsuit show of the 1960s was again realized in Hollywood, though not exclusively in publicity shots. A teen-something generation of baby-boomers grew up with movies that took every opportunity to show young bodies in swimsuits, whether in the Hawaiian locales of Elvis Presley films or the beach-blanket high jinks of films featuring Annette Funicello and Frankie Avalon. Often Hollywood used clothing to convey the subtle message that nice girls wear maillots and bad girls wear bikinis. Correspondingly, the good guys wore puffy boxers in plain colors and cabana sets, while the bad guys mixed sportswear and even motorcycle jackets with their beachwear. By decade's end, nice girls were clearly finishing last as the former isolation of scant bikinis to a few conspicuous European beaches gave way to mass adoption in America. For men, trunks and boxers were means to neutralize anatomy; sleek racing trunks and bikinis were widely worn in America only in the 1970s.

But what most prominently separated modesty from novelty in the 1960s was Rudi Gernreich's 1964 "topless" bathing suit, or monokini, as the Europeans called it, an extreme form that galvanized public opinion and garnered extraordinary press coverage. Although only a vanguard was ready to accept Gernreich's more-or-less theoretical premise, the liberated 1960s were willing to carry into a new decade the possibilities of bathing apparel that skimped more and more, not only for women, but also in the increasingly brief swimming apparel of men as well.

If virtually every inch of the body was visible at one time or another in the 1970s, an analogous exploration of mood and narrative animated swimwear photography. Helmut Newton's alternately mysterious, mischievous, misogynic, and masochistic photographs of swimwear delighted in the bathing suit as a commonplace and a paranudity, while Bill King's photographs splashed with real-life wetness and youthful *joie de vivre*. For these photographers, the swimsuit was tantamount to nakedness, its presence in the photograph giving a touch of legitimacy and a larger element of license and libido. To be sure, in the cultural context of *Hair* (1967) and *Oh! Calcutta!* (1969–89), there were many—quite often puerile—experiments with the body and nudity on dry land; swimwear was not only a danger zone, but an avant-garde zone as well. Likewise, Oliviero Toscani's underwater images might have served as the denouement of E. L. Doctorow's *World's Fair* (1985), and Hiro's animated pictures of swimming captured the candor and the moment that had heretofore twinkled for Munkacsi. A Rico Puhlmann photograph of 1975 epitomizes the narrative insinuation of the decade in reflecting sunglasses hooked into the back of a bikini bottom, thereby calling further attention (as if it could pass unnoticed) to the ring that encircles flesh at the base of the spine. The glasses involve the viewer in converse spectatorship, but also in the casual carrying of accessories on a body so barely clad. Parkinson, Toscani, and other photographers of the 1970s chose models with the same cultural and racial diversity as that of models of drier fashion.

ABOVE:
Featured in a roundup of "Fibers of 1953," navy-blue Lastex bathing suit, woven of Chromspun acetate, by Flexees. Photograph by Louise Dahl-Wolfe. Published *Harper's Bazaar*, May 1953. Courtesy Staley-Wise Gallery.

OPPOSITE:
Marilyn Monroe, 1949. Photograph by André de Dienes. Courtesy Mrs. André de Dienes and Éditions Filipacchi.

FOLLOWING PAGES:
Left to right: Maillot by Arabel, men's shorts by Rasurel, maillot by Ariella, maillot by Loris Azzaro. Photograph by Helmut Newton. Published French *Vogue*, April 1978. Courtesy the photographer and Publications Condé Nast, S.A.

ABOVE:
Terri May on the beach at Saint
Croix. Photograph by Norman
Parkinson. Published *Town and
Country*, May 1987. Courtesy
Hamiltons Photographers.

OPPOSITE:
Iman at King Peter's Bay, Tobago,
wearing loop of white Hurel jersey,
by Shuji Tojo. Photograph by
Norman Parkinson. Published
British *Vogue*, 1976. Courtesy
Condé Nast Publications, Inc.

RIGHT:
Jersey suit and straw hat by Jacques Heim. Photograph by Jean Moral. Published *Harper's Bazaar*, June 1935. Courtesy The Hearst Corporation.

OPPOSITE:
On the beach in California. Ribcord swimsuit of cotton, rayon, and Lastex yarn, by Jantzen. Photograph by Louise Dahl-Wolfe. Published *Harper's Bazaar*, May 1948. Courtesy The Hearst Corporation.

BELOW:
The Japanese influence: bathing suit by Carolyn Schnurer. Photograph by Louise Dahl-Wolfe. Published *Harper's Bazaar*, January 1952. Courtesy The Hearst Corporation.

OPPOSITE:
Maillot by Catalina. Photograph by
Arthur Elgort. Published American
Vogue, January 1976. Courtesy
Condé Nast Publications, Inc.

RIGHT:
Gold lamé and velvet bikini by Yves
Saint Laurent Beachwear.
Photograph by Bill King. Published
American *Vogue,* January 1987.
Courtesy Condé Nast Publications,
Inc.

Mark Spitz and friend, who wears a
white tank suit by Rudi Gernreich
for Harmon Knitwear. Photograph
by Bill King. Published *Harper's
Bazaar*, May 1970. Courtesy Janet
McClelland and The Hearst
Corporation.

FITNESS AND THE NEW PHYSIQUE

Characteristic of the models of the decade is their well-toned and defined musculature, and swimwear presented the perfect showcase for strength combined with beauty. Bared thighs in high-cut suits and ultimately, in the mid-1970s, thong styles, required the most athletic appearance, one that would have daunted or compromised most earlier swimsuit models. What *Sports Illustrated* demanded of models in its frankly exploitative swimwear issues was a genuine sports type, something subtly differentiated from a pornographic ideal, yet equally and aggressively erotic. This evolution of a natural American beauty—ever a good girl—was of a kind with the decade's growing interest in women in sports, with emphasis on gymnastics and swimming, both of which demand body suits that allow maximum motion. It took fifty years until the sports paradigms that emancipated men from restrictive sporting clothing in the 1930s were effective for women, but in the decade of the 1970s women too expressed themselves as the jocks that men had long been. Their equity is epitomized in an Arthur Elgort photograph (*Vogue,* July 1976), in which the female bather is now borne, divine and exuberant, above the sputtering head of her male carrier. A picture of Mark Spitz before winning gold medals at the 1972 Olympics in Munich represented the male swimmer as something more than a vacant Hollywood convention (though Spitz momentarily strove for the recognition that had been accorded to Johnny Weissmuller and Buster Crabbe). The female swimmer, likewise, was a wonder woman, an extraordinary athlete, no passive idyll of the male gaze. When, in 1984, Raquel Welch posed for Bill King with the Olympic swim team, the elements were familiar: erotic charge, the female as full athletic and aerobic partner and participant, and the interplay of nudity and swimwear.

In the 1980s swimwear imagery continued to demand action, adventure, and bodies built not from sandy repose but from arduous exercise and regimen. Indeed, as sports photography took more and more of its cues from the wide world of television, the physical ideal became remorselessly vigorous and conditioned. The ideal body type has changed throughout history in both art and fashion. The buxom postwar ideal was successively supplanted by skinny Twiggy, then highly conditioned Cheryl Tiegs. From the perspective of the 1980s, much of the earlier swimwear modelling may seem flaccid and romantically soft.

As for the bathing costumes, even a Weissmuller would think men's racing trunks today only the internal element of a swim outfit, while an Annette Kellerman would blush at the reduction of women's attire to similarly basic elements. Fashion photography has responded with the adulation of the physique, whether in photographs of Lisa Lyons as bodybuilder or in the muscular studies that intrigued photographers of the 1980s, including Ritts, Weber, and Robert Mapplethorpe. The geography, the shoreline, and other interests of swimwear photography have changed—indeed, such preoccupations are as mutable